Folens

Poetry Works

Pupil Book 1 – Teacher Notes

Mary Green

Folens books are protected by international copyright laws. All rights reserved. The copyright of all materials in this book, except where otherwise stated, remains the property of the publisher and author. No part of this publication may be reproduced, stored in a retrieval system, or transmitted, in any form or by any means, for whatever purpose, without the written permission of Folens Limited.

Folens allow photocopying of pages marked 'copiable page' for educational use, providing that this use is within the confines of the purchasing institution. Copiable pages should not be declared in respect of any photocopying licence.

Mary Green hereby asserts her moral right to be identified as the author of this work in accordance with the Copyright, Designs and Patents Act 1988.

Additional poems by Mary Green.

Editor: Gaynor Spry   Layout artist: James Brown   Cover design: Martin Cross

© 2000 Folens Limited, on behalf of the author.

First published 2000 by Folens Limited, Albert House, Apex Business Centre, Boscombe Road, Dunstable, LU5 4RL, England.

ISBN 1 84163 690-8

Printed in Singapore by Craft Print.

Contents

Introduction 4
Correlation chart 5

Guided Group Work

Part 1
Song 6
What is Sharp? 7
Nature Shapes 8
Up the Stairs to Bed! 9
Fish 10
Crescent Moon 10
Animal Sneezes 11
Caribbean 12

Part 2
Chinese New Year in China Town 13
Diwali 14

Part 3
Bubble Trouble 15
Says of the Week 16
Eyes Bigger Than … 17
It's Not Fair 18
Feet 18
The Wise Young Owl 19
A Shaggy Dog Story 20

Using the Activity Sheets: Part 1 21
Lemon Lollipops (alliteration, the senses) 23
Like Playing Ships (similes) 24
The Jelly-Bus (hyphens) 25
Beautiful Letters (calligrams, shape poems) 26
Spin Me a Rhyme (rhyme) 27
No! (punctuation) 28
Four Creatures (riddles) 29

Using the Activity Sheets: Part 2 30
Animal Acrostics (acrostics) 32
Tapping Out the Beat (syllables) 33
Stressing the Words (stress) 34
Going With the Flow (beat, syllables) 35
Finding the Best Voice (rhythm) 36
What a Performance! (performance poetry) 37
What is Spiky? (adjectives) 38

Using the Activity Sheets: Part 3 39
Making Tongue Twisters (alliteration) 41
Using Sounds Carefully (alliteration) 42
Only Joking! (jokes) 43
Silly Sounds (onomatopoeia) 44
Loves Hates Always Never (nonsense poems) 45
Which is Which? (poetic forms) 46
The Owl and the Pussy-Cat (classic poem) 47

Sound patterns and metre 48

Introduction

Poetry Works Pupil Books provide well-structured and lively activities to allow children to work independently through a wide range of contemporary and classic poetry. Every effort has been made to produce lively and interesting books, in the belief that poetry should be an exciting experience. Not only are the children encouraged to play with language, but also to read poetry for the sheer pleasure of the words.

Book 1 addresses:

Part 1   poems based on observation and the senses; shape poems
Part 2   oral and performance poetry from different cultures
Part 3   humorous poetry, poetry that plays with language.

Each Pupil Book follows a common format. There are four pages to a section organised under these headings:

Thinking and talking
Here the children are asked to discuss a poem, with a partner or in a group, or to think about it on their own, at your discretion.

Tasks
These involve written or other activities and are occasionally an extension of discussion work. The tasks give practice in technique and other aspects of poetry and allow children to play with words and consider wider possibilities. The activities culminate in the writing of poems or other types of work.

Follow-up
A further poem or poems linked to the first (and sometimes written by a child) is included here with extension activities, often covering display or research work.

Keywords and Glossary
Keywords are listed within each section and can be found in the Glossary.

About the poet
Information is included on the poets who have written the main poems of the section.

These Teacher Notes provide:

Correlation chart
The main types of poem and features covered in each chapter are referenced in the correlation chart.

Guided group work
This section offers help with both guided reading and writing.

Guided reading
Brief suggestions on how to approach the reading of a text are given here. These ideas follow on from the activities offered to the children in the Pupil Book, either developing the work or introducing new approaches.

Guided writing
Most tasks in the Pupil Book are addressed in this section, except where research or display work are involved (usually the final task in each section). *Note: When discussing techniques or devices, such as alliteration or rhyme, ensure that the children understand that these devices are used to add meaning and give order to a poem. They are not ends in themselves.*

Activity sheets
The photocopiable activity sheets are split into three sections and can be used to support the tasks for each part of the Pupil Book. Advice is given on using the activity sheets.

Sound patterns and metre
This reference sheet, designed for the teacher, gives information on sound patterns and metre in English poetry.

Poetry Works posters
Many of the poems studied in the Pupil Books and further additional poems are available as posters. Each poster pack is accompanied by Teacher Notes, giving an in-depth guide to every poem and providing suggestions for using the poems in whole-class shared work.

Range of poems and technical terms covered in Pupil Book 1

Please note: Poetry forms are shown in bold.

	Song (4–7)	What is Sharp? (8–11)	Nature Shapes (12–15)	Up the Stairs to Bed! (16–19)	Fish/Crescent Moon (20–23)	Animal Sneezes (24–27)	Caribbean (28–31)	Chinese New Year (32–35)	Diwali (36–39)	Bubble Trouble (40–43)	Says of the Week (44–47)	Eyes Bigger Than ... (48–51)	It's Not Fair/Feet (52–55)	The Wise Young Owl (56–59)	A Shaggy Dog Story (60–63)
acrostic							●								
adjective		●						●							
alliteration										●	●		●		
calligram				●											
comic verse										●	●				
dash			●												
dictionary work		●		●		●		●							
exclamation mark			●		●										
hyphen			●												●
image								●	●						
joke											●				
list poem														●	
nonsense verse														●	●
noun		●													
observation	●	●	●												
onomatopoeia								●		●		●			
paragraph				●											
performance poem							●	●	●			●			
phrase	●	●	●				●								
poetry related to other cultures							●	●	●						
prefixes														●	
question and answer poem		●					●								
question mark		●					●								
repeating pattern		●						●	●				●		
rhyme	●	●	●						●			●		●	
rhythm									●						
senses	●	●													
shape poem				●	●			●							
simile			●												
story					●										●
stress									●	●					
syllable									●						
synonym						●									
thesaurus work						●			●						
tongue twister										●	●				
verb	●									●			●		
word association															●
word play										●	●				
writing frame															●

Guided Group Work

Song by Mary Green (Pupil Book pages 4–7)

What the Children Need to Know

- The relationship between expression and meaning when reading poetry and the importance of listening both to their own voices and to others
- There can be a relationship between the sound of a word and its meaning (onomatopoeia)
- What rhyme is and how it can be used to create effects
- The part that observation and the senses can play in poetry
- How powerful verbs can be used to create effects

Preparation for Guided Reading

Song page 4

- Focus on the pace and pauses in 'Song', noting in particular that the pause before the final line on each verse helps to sum up its meaning.
- Ask different children to read the verses and emphasise listening skills both to the reader and to the listeners.
- The children can read the poem together, synchronising their voices and giving expression to the meaning of the poem.

On the Wind of January page 7

- This is a good winter verse that sticks in the mind and is reminiscent of a playground chant for cold days. Ask the children to recite it again and again and listen to its lilt.
- The children should note where the verse pauses, the run-on lines and the way the final line slows, announcing the wind.

Preparation for Guided Writing

Task A

- Emphasise the relationship between the choice of words in 'Song' and spring.
- Encourage the children to share the words they have chosen and contributed and to give reasons for their choice before writing.
- Include work on the words that do not suit spring and what they conjure up. The children can also write down their own similar-sounding words and definitions.

Task B

- Word chains are useful for highlighting rhyme.
- Note which children experience difficulty in identifying rhyming words.
- Add non-rhyming words later.

Task C

- Ask the children to find words that sum up the end of summer, heralding autumn (e.g. words related to the end of the school holidays). They can record the best.
- Ensure the children understand the meaning of 'yearning' before beginning Task C.

Task D

- The children can write down other verbs related to winter, e.g. skate/skating, tobogganing.
- The poem 'Song' relies heavily on the present participle 'ing'. See Using the Activity Sheets, *Like Playing Ships*, for a discussion of this.

Task E

- Focus on the lines given to help the children begin a poem or discuss additional ideas, such as squirrels gathering nuts, gusty days, the silence of snow.
- The children may prefer to use a verse from 'Song' or 'On the Wind of January' as a model.
- The poem can be completed during independent work or extended writing.

Guided Group Work

What is Sharp? *by John Foster (Pupil Book pages 8–11)*

What the Children Need to Know

- The usefulness of listening to others read
- What the senses are
- How to identify words that evoke the senses and distinguish between them
- How to use a dictionary
- What nouns and adjectives are and how they work together
- How poetry conjures up pictures in the mind and that these pictures (images) can represent other things

Preparation for Guided Reading

What is Sharp? *page 9*

- Note that the poem starts with a question and that this will affect how the title is read.
- Point out that there are full stops at the end of each line, and that the poem is rather like a list poem, except for the organisation of the verses.
- Note that most lines stop 'sharply'. This, of course, suits the meaning of the poem.
- Ask the children, before they start reading, how the second verse differs in punctuation.
- Note that the use of the indefinite article 'A', along with the last two lines of the second verse, speeds up the poem. This could be reflected in the reading.
- Ask the children to comment on the reading of the final verse (which slows down).
- The children could take turns to read the poem and listen to each other.

Soft is its Fur *page 11*

- Ask the children to say how they would read the verse. (It has a bouncy rhythm, partly due to the repetition, and should be easy to remember.)
- The first and third lines include 'is its', while the second and fourth only 'its'. This can be tricky to say. Note whether the children omit 'is'.
- The verse is a simple riddle and could be read with a touch of mystery.
- You might also wish to read the complete poem with the children. See activity sheet *Four Creatures*, relating this to Task F in the Pupil Book.

Preparation for Guided Writing

Task A

- Before the children use a dictionary, they could write down the meanings of any unfamiliar words by thinking about their sounds (such as 'fang'). A useful lesson in the way meaning is conveyed by sound!

Task B

- Other ways to explore the meaning of 'sharp' might be through the remaining senses: a sharp taste/smell/noise.

Task C

- Ask the children to write down their own concrete examples of what 'soft' and 'tingling' mean. These might have personal connotations and can be contrasted with 'sharp'.
- When completing Task C2, prompt the children to visualise situations that suit the words. This encourages their imaginations and can be a revelation to them.

Task D

- Remind the children of the relationship between nouns and adjectives.
- Explore unusual noun/adjective combinations (a 'cunning' arrow) and ask the children to devise their poems in light of this.

Task E

- The work already done should encourage the children to recognise that images can represent objects.

Guided Group Work

Nature Shapes by Sue Cowling (Pupil Book pages 12–15)

What the Children Need to Know

- Timing and pace are important in poetry
- The importance of observation
- What dashes and exclamations are and how they affect expression
- How hyphens can be used to create new words
- 'Like' and 'as' are useful words for comparing things

Preparation for Guided Reading

Nature Shapes page 13

- Read the poem to the children, stressing the dash and the exclamation mark each time. (The poem is so vivid you can hardly do otherwise.)
- Discuss the meaning of unfamiliar words such as 'tendrils'.
- Ask the children how they think the dashes and exclamation marks affect the poem and discuss other examples of their use in everyday conversation.
- A group of four children could practise the poem, reading a verse each. They would need to read each verse quickly and also observe cues between verses, which alert them to the importance of timing.

No! page 15

- This verse from the poem by Thomas Hood also uses the dash and exclamation mark to create excitement. The use of repetition encourages a sense of urgency. The children should hardly pause after the commas, but should accentuate the pause after the dashes.
- Discuss with them the relationship between 'No' and 'November!'.
- The complete poem (which is challenging for children of this age) is available as the activity sheet *No!* for those who might be interested. Some children might like to read it to each other.

Preparation for Guided Writing

Task A

- Provide detailed illustrations of 'horns, beaks and claws' and other features for the children to observe, e.g. woodcuts by the German artist Dürer.
- The children could draw their own ideas of 'horns, beaks and claws', or any other examples from the poem, and discuss their shapes before beginning Task A.

Task B

- The use of the words 'like' and 'as' is discussed as preparation for the term 'simile'. This term is referred to in *Poetry Works* Pupil Book 2, but you might wish to introduce it here.
- Encourage unusual comparisons, e.g. 'a necklace like a trickle of tears' rather than 'rain/raindrops'.

Task C

- The hyphen is a wonderful invention! It encourages a leap of imagination and allows us to describe or define something when we are lost for words. All the examples here can be combined in different ways. The children can discuss the meanings of their words before beginning Task C3.

Task D

- When the children write similes, encourage the use of alliteration, as in 'thousand thundering'. (The term alliteration does not have to be used.) Alliteration comes easily to children who will use it in play or 'silly' conversation with friends.

Task E

- Further extension work using the word 'Maybe' as a starter word could be developed here. It would be quite different in tone to the 'No!' and 'Yes!' poems.
- All the poems could be included in the folder and used as a resource in the classroom.

Guided Group Work

Up the Stairs to Bed! *by Ian Souter (Pupil Book pages 16–19)*

What the Children Need to Know

- What a shape poem is and how it can be expressed in various ways
- How letters can be played with to make shapes
- The relationship between meaning and layout in a poem
- How feelings are evoked in shape poems
- What calligrams are
- What a paragraph is

Preparation for Guided Reading

Up the Stairs to Bed! *page 16*

- The main focus here is the slow, sleepy voice with which the reader 'climbs the stairs'. Discuss how the children could make their voices sound progressively slower. Then point to the visual impact of the poem and its relationship to the reading of it.
- Point out that the repetition of the word 'so' accentuates the sleepy tone of the poem.
- The children could end the word 'asleep' with a yawn.

Tick-Tock *page 19*

- You might wish to discuss why children dislike the idea of bedtime and what the 'nine o'clock watershed' is.
- Ask the children in what tone they would read the mother's comment to the child.
- Point out how the heavy rhyme accentuates the mother's voice.

Preparation for Guided Writing

Task A

- Ask the children what they think the pictures represent in each word and, where appropriate, what letter they replace.
- Discuss how the letters 's' in 'snake', 'o' in 'spot' and 'e' in 'eyes' lend themselves easily to representation.

Task B

- Use the example 'jumping down' at the top of page 16 to reinforce the relationship between meaning and layout.
- You might need to discuss the importance of representing the verbs carefully so that the layout is clear. (There is an art to even the simplest shape poem!) The children might need to practise writing the words until they are satisfied.
- The children could display their finished poems, and discuss the range of interpretation.

Task C

- This task is trickier still. If the children can capture the essence of the word (so, for example, the word 'crouch' is written in very small letters) they will have understood the task.

Task D

- A tactile experience here (using fingers to creep up the stairs of the poem) can reinforce meaning.
- Discuss several instances of 'falling asleep' and the consequences, e.g. missing your bus-stop.

Task E

- The children might be able to generate several 'sleepy' poems from the words and poem suggested and from their own paragraphs.
- Encourage the children to choose lines which can be presented visually, e.g. in the shape of a television set, or as rows of heads in assembly (the poem could be depicted as a wavy line amongst a sea of heads).

Task F

- This task is useful both for encouraging children to revise their work and for incorporating shape words and calligrams in a single poem.
- All the words suggested have at least one letter that can be presented clearly in picture form, e.g. shOuts/shOUts.

Guided Group Work

Fish *by Ruth Underhill*
Crescent Moon *by Sue Cowling (Pupil Book pages 20–23)*

What the Children Need to Know

- A shape poem is like a puzzle and might contain a hidden story
- An understanding of the relationship between layout, words and meaning
- A shape can suggest more than one thing and there are many kinds of shape poems
- Feelings are evoked by shape poems
- How to use a dictionary

Preparation for Guided Reading

Fish *page 21*

- Ask the children to begin reading the poem alone from 'Splish Splash …'. They could also read the poem from the bottom up, starting 'Wiggly Worm …'.
- Prompt the children to accentuate 'The End' either by saying it either more loudly or in a whisper. You might also wish to point out the use of alliteration.

Crescent Moon *page 21*

- As the children read 'Crescent Moon' ask them what shape their eyes trace out as they follow the poem.
- Note where the pauses come and how the rhyme helps to close the poem.

Heart *page 23*

- Ask the children what shape their eyes trace out as they read 'Heart'.
- Check they understand that the poem is a flame when read upside down. You can also point out the words 'same as a flame' in the poem.

Preparation for Guided Writing

Task A

- This poem forms the perfect shape of a fish, which adds to its meaning.
- Discuss the story in 'Fish', pointing out that 'End' is both the end of the fish and the end of the story. Consider the subtle changes in meaning if the poem is read from the bottom up.

Task B

- The children could look closely at the apple and write down the repeating line 'ripe apple, rosy apple …', discussing why it is the key to the story.

Task C

- 'The silver hook' is a metaphor. It is not suggested that the term is used here, but it might be useful to ensure the children know what 'The silver hook' represents (and why it is like the crescent moon).

Task D

- Once the children have identified the common word 'hook' in 'Crescent Moon' and 'Fish', discuss its relevance in both poems. Emphasise to the children that they are solving puzzles.

Task E

- Here the children are encouraged to look at a similar shape from a different perspective. 'Boomerang' also tells a story. Ask the children what it is.

Task F

- The smiley badge might have personal connotations for the children. They could share their words with each other, or make lists together, selecting some words and rejecting others. They could use dictionaries to help them.

Task G

- This task encourages observation. Ask the children to collect similar shapes to the crescent moon, e.g. the letter 'C', the handle of a cup.

Task H

- When the children understand how 'Heart' works, ask them how the poem makes them feel. Prompt them to make the association between 'heart' and 'flame'.
- Ask them who they would give the poem to and why.

Guided Group Work

Animal Sneezes by Roger Stevens (Pupil Book pages 24–27)

What the Children Need to Know

- Sound can be expressed visually and used in shape poems
- How variation in the voice can shift meaning
- What a question mark is and that questions can be asked in poetry
- What a synonym is
- What a thesaurus is and its usefulness when reading and writing poetry

Preparation for Guided Reading

Animal Sneezes page 25

- The children can read the poem in a variety of ways. The first four lines can be read in a matter-of-fact manner, with 'atishoo' as a throwaway line, but with greater variation as the poem proceeds. Or they can vary the expression and sound of 'atishoo' throughout, according to the animal.

The Answers page 27

- The children can read this poem in numerous ways, e.g. as partners, with one asking the questions, the other the statements, in the first three verses; or reading a verse each in the first three verses, then reading the final verse together with greater emphasis.
- When asking the question, show them how to give a quizzical expression to the voice or one of mock-seriousness.

Preparation for Guided Writing

Task A

- Discuss the variation in sound in a range of animal sneezes and encourage the children to share their ideas before they start writing.
- Encourage them to relate shape to sound, e.g. a snake sneezing.

Task B

- You could also discuss how different people or even objects, such as a clock, might snore and laugh.
- Ask the children to think of words as well as sounds for snoring and laughing, referring to a thesaurus for synonyms if necessary. They can incorporate words into their 'sound shapes' as illustrated on page 24 of the Pupil Book.

Task C

- Although onomatopoeia is not mentioned here, you might wish to introduce the term.
- Play games in which each child performs the actions and sounds of common tasks, e.g. cleaning their teeth, while the others guess what the task is. Then ask them to express the sound in words.

Task D

- Ask the children to consider how they will end their poems and what punctuation they will use.
- They could leave out what the object is, turning the poem into a riddle. The last line could be 'What am I?'

Task E

- Collect a selection of contrary or 'child-like' questions, e.g. Why is the grass green?
- Ask the children to consider how unusual animals would answer, e.g. a duck-billed platypus.

Guided Group Work

Caribbean *by Anita Marie Sackett (Pupil Book pages 28–31)*

What the Children Need to Know

- What an acrostic is
- How an acrostic can vary
- How poetry creates word pictures (images)
- What a performance poem is
- How you might combine words to create images and feelings
- How to use a thesaurus

Preparation for Guided Reading

Caribbean *page 29*

- Prompt the children to note the pauses as they read. Point out that most commas come after the words which make up the acrostic.
- Note that the additional rhyme 'oo' in the last line encourages the voice to draw to a close. ('Bloom/moon' is an example of assonance, where the medial vowels rhyme but the end consonants do not.)
- There are also suggestions for performing the poem in Task D.

Sunbeam *page 31*

- Point out that there is no punctuation in this acrostic.
- Ask the children how they would read the poem and what impression this gives.
- Ask them what else, apart from the lack of punctuation, encourages the poem to be read quickly. (The poem uses double rhyme, which you might like to mention.)
- The children should also consider how the reading is linked to the poem's meaning.

Preparation for Guided Writing

Task A

- The children can begin by discussing the images in 'Caribbean' or by looking around for examples, e.g. 'cloudless sky', before making colour word sums.

Task B

- It is useful to have a thesaurus to hand, so that the children can collect relevant words, e.g. abstract nouns.
- Ask the children to make a list of abstract nouns to match their word sums and then ask questions, such as: What are the colours of speed? youth? kindness? Prompt them to match colours in unusual ways.

Task C

- Emphasise the relationship between the meaning of the acrostic and the rest of the poem. Writing an acrostic using a lengthy word is trickier than it appears. The vowels can sometimes prove difficult. Encourage short words initially.
- Using letters from parts of the word other than the beginning (as shown in 'red') is a useful way to begin writing acrostics – reading down is emphasised and acrostics in this form are easier to complete. You could ask each child to write short acrostics, in this way, related to other colours.

Task D

- You might like to include drums in the performance of 'Caribbean', which maintain the rhythm of the poem as the children say it.

Task E

- You could ask the children to imagine a mirror and also the reflections they might see in water.
- Ask them to imagine sunbeams coming together to form a reflection.
- Help the children to collect suitable words for the additional line beginning with 's'. They could continue the pattern of the poem – using two words – or break the pattern and write a longer line.

Guided Group Work – Part 2

Chinese New Year in China Town

by Andrew Collett (Pupil Book pages 32–35)

What the Children Need to Know

- What a syllable is
- Begin to understand what stress in a poem is
- How to read a poem without overstressing the beat (unless it is a specific feature of a performance)
- How to make word pictures (images)
- What adjectives are and their usefulness in poetry
- Different ways of performing a poem

Preparation for Guided Reading

Chinese New Year in China Town
page 33

- Ask the children to shut their eyes and imagine the scene while you read the poem.
- Point out where the punctuation is.
- Ask the children to read the verses to you as a group. (The poem has pace and the lines are short.)
- Now read the poem to them again. This time you could lay the stress on different words.
- See suggestions for performing the poem in Task D on page 34 of the Pupil Book.

Sampan *page 35*

- Point out to the children that there is no punctuation in the poem.
- See suggestions for reading and performing the poem given in Task E on page 35 of the Pupil Book.
- Please note 'Sampan' is reprinted on the activity sheet *Going With the Flow*.

Preparation for Guided Writing

Task A

- To help the children think of adjectives, before turning to a thesaurus, suggest they think of alliterative words, e.g. 'flashing firecracker', 'fire-lit faces', 'demon drums'.
- The children might wish to use repeating images to make the dragon's tail.
- They could combine images, to make a communal poem, or write a poem in pairs.

Task B

- Discuss the form the children's 'celebration' poems will take, e.g. repeated lines as shown.
- Some children might wish to incorporate the images from Task A.

Task C

- To understand the difference between syllables and words in poetry the children need to tap out the beat. However, this can give the impression that poetry should be read in a stilted fashion! While it is not suggested that metre is discussed here, you might wish to explain that in English poetry some syllables will be stressed, while others will be unstressed. Generally speaking, the children should be encouraged to read the poem naturally, trusting their own voices.
- There is a series of activity sheets in this book to help with these points: *Tapping Out the Beat, Stressing the Words, Going With the Flow, Finding the Best Voice*, and *What a Performance!*

Tasks D and E

- You might wish to give the children guidance about what shape their performance will take, e.g. the kind of actions they could perform, and what instruments are available, before they begin Tasks D and E.

Guided Group Work – Part 2

Diwali *by David Harmer (Pupil Book pages 36–39)*

What the Children Need to Know

- What Diwali is
- The importance of light at Diwali
- What rhythm is
- The difference between rhythm and rhyme
- The story of Rama and Sita
- Different ways of performing a poem
- How to see word pictures (images) and create them

Preparation for Guided Reading

Diwali *page 36*

- The poem moves urgently and there is little punctuation. It has a strong rhythmic chant. This suits the idea of banishing darkness. Ask the children to try reading the poem as a group or in pairs.
- Discuss where they think the poem should be stressed.
- See suggestions for performing the poem in Task D on page 38 of the Pupil Book.

Water *page 39*

- There are many pauses in this poem and yet it has speed. This creates the impression of water darting everywhere, except in the line 'waves whispering'. Ask the children how they would read it and where they would lay the stress.
- See suggestions for reading and performing the poem in Task E on page 39 of the Pupil Book.

Preparation for Guided Writing

Task A

- Discuss with the children why the poem captures the essence of Diwali, who Rama and Sita are and what has been driven away. (Diwali is a principal Hindu festival held in October/November. Light returns and darkness is driven out. Rama is the hero of the *Ramayana*. He and his wife Sita are reunited, symbolising the perfect marriage. Lakshmi, the goddess of prosperity, is also important at Diwali.)
- The children should try Tasks A1, 2 and 3, using additional words to give them practice in seeing and making images.
- Repetition is important in the poem. The children could choose a particular word or phrase to repeat in their own poems, or use 'light' as suggested.

Task B

- This is a more complicated image. The children could imitate the metaphor 'the mountains wept in waterfalls' to produce the 'tears of the sun' and so on.
- The children are also encouraged to use similes in Task B2. The term is introduced in the activity sheet *Like Playing Ships,* and you might wish to discuss it.

Task C

- Ask the children what they think rhyme is, giving examples.
- Ask them what they think rhythm is.
- Ensure they understand the difference between rhythm and rhyme.
- Explain that the two can work together to form a poem.

Tasks D and E

- These tasks are concerned with reading and performance. You might wish to use the activity sheet *What a Performance!* in conjunction with these tasks.

Guided Group Work – Part 3

Bubble Trouble by Ian Souter (Pupil Book pages 40–43)

What the Children Need to Know

- What double rhyme is
- What alliteration is
- What a tongue twister is
- How to lay out a recipe using instructional language (imperative verbs)
- The words in a tongue twister start with the same sound (alliteration)

Preparation for Guided Reading

Bubble Trouble page 41

- You could read this free verse poem to the children as though you were explaining an incident or potential crisis, so that you accentuate the pauses. The poem has a conversational style.
- Alternatively, you could read the poem as a tongue twister, ignoring most of the pauses. (You could, of course, read it both ways.)

The Frog page 43

- The poem compels us to read it with a London or South-East accent. The repetition also accentuates the cadence of ordinary speech. (Those children who watch *EastEnders* are likely to recognise the accent immediately.) Others might need some help.
- You might, therefore, wish to read the poem to the children initially. Before you begin, ask them to visualise a frog. (The illustration in the Pupil Book should help.)
- Ask them to note where you pause and the sense of amazement in your voice.

Preparation for Guided Writing

Task A

- Provide the children with single and double rhymes and ask them to distinguish between the two. The vowels and consonants should be the same in the double rhymes, e.g. 'puddle', 'muddle', 'cuddle', 'huddle'; 'kitten', 'mitten'. You might like to point out that two words can work together to make a double rhyme: 'kick it', 'ticket'.

Task B

- Ask the children what other descriptive names they can think of for 'tongue twister', e.g. 'lip curler', 'face wobbler'.

Task C

- Practise alliteration with the children, asking them to think of other words that start with 'gl'.
- You could also practise using other consonant alliteration: 'b', 'l', 'p', 's', 'sw', 't' and 'w'. Ask the children for alliterative words using vowels, e.g. 'Eddie Edwards ate Ernie Edwards' eggs'. (It is the consonants that give the most trouble!)

Task D

- The children should know how to use instructional language to write the recipe poem. It is not necessary to discuss the term 'imperative', but suggest they begin each line with a verb.
- You might wish to add more lines to the example given: 'Stew stars in …', 'Stir stones in …'.
- Encourage the children to find other alliterative words.

Task E

- This poem shows nicely how grammatical rules can be muddled and how slang can be used for poetic ends. It also illustrates how nonsense can have its own logic. However, it is difficult to write such poems successfully! The model provided will allow the children to focus on ideas to suit each creature.
- Discuss the relationship between the creatures and a bird, e.g. through movement and flight. You might wish to add other examples, e.g. a kite, a paper plane, a frisbee.

15

Guided Group Work

Says of the Week by John Foster (Pupil Book pages 44–47)

What the Children Need to Know

- What a play on words is
- How jokes often use this device
- How 'Knock, knock' jokes work
- What a tongue twister is

Preparation for Guided Reading

Says of the Week page 45

- Read the poem to the children.
- Point out the punctuation, particularly the full stops which divide the poem in half. (This device is called caesura – from the Latin 'to cut'.)
- Ask the children to read the poem, individually or with another child. They should identify the days of the week before they begin.
- If working with partners, one child could read the first half of the line and the other child the second half, to emphasise the play on words.

Days of the Week page 47

- Point out where the run-on lines are and where the full stops come.
- Note the regular rhythm, the extra beats in line seven and the way the rhythm is broken in line eleven, leading to the close in line twelve.
- The poem divides clearly into three parts. A trio could read it, taking a part each.

Whether the Weather be Hot page 47

- Read this well-known rhyme to the children quickly. Appear to struggle in parts to emphasise the 'tongue-twisting' nature of the poem!

Preparation for Guided Writing

Task A

- The jokes are tricky. Ensure the children understand how the poem works before they begin Task A, referring back to Preparation for Guided Reading above if necessary.

Task B

- This task should help the children see the relationship between the days of the week and the play on words. There are two words that can be chosen for each day as follows: Moanday, Mandyday; Chewsday, Trueday; Whenday, Winnie's day; Terseday, Burstday; Fliesday, Flierday; Setterday, Scatterday; Sumday, Sunbedday.
- The children might need to use a dictionary for any words they don't know.

Task C

- Ask the children to explain how the 'Knock, knock' jokes work, before they attempt their own. (Sometimes they will laugh because it sounds funny, without fully understanding the joke!)

Task D

- This poem should provide clues about the meaning of 'Says of the Week' for any child who has not yet grasped the play on words!
- Discuss which days of the week and of the year are the children's favourites and why.

Task E

- Ask the children to explain what a tongue twister is and why it is a suitable term for 'Whether the Weather be Hot'.

Guided Group Work

Eyes Bigger Than ... by Mike Johnson (Pupil Book pages 48–51)

What the Children Need to Know

- The relationship between sound and meaning
- Some words sound like their meaning
- The meaning of 'onomatopoeia'
- How to classify sounds
- How to create new onomatopoeic words
- Different ways of performing a poem
- Using rhyme can create effects
- Repetition can be used to create humour

Preparation for Guided Reading

Eyes Bigger Than ... page 49

- The main rhyme here is double and internal.
- The repetition of the double rhymes and the use of onomatopoeia help to drive the forceful rhythm along so that the poem sounds like its meaning. Read the poem to the children, accentuating this.

Jelly on a Plate page 51

- This playground chant has a similar quality to 'Eyes Bigger Than ...'.
- The children could read the poem as a group with vigour and pace.

Preparation for Guided Writing

Task A

- The children should have received sufficient clues from the reading and discussion above to have worked out the answers.

Task B

- The children are asked to identify 'light' as well as 'heavy' sounds, as contrast. This also helps to reinforce what onomatopoeia is.
- Encourage the children to read the words aloud before classifying them.
- Leave checking any words the children do not understand until they have completed the tasks, so that, as far as possible, they respond to the sound of the words initially.

Task C

- Discuss the suggestions in Task C with the children. Ensure they settle on an idea for their poem with you and discuss the vocabulary they might use.

Task D

- 'Eyes Bigger Than ...' is a good poem to perform. Apart from the suggestions in the Pupil Book some children might be able to organise themselves into two groups and rehearse the poem as an a cappella group, or along the lines of a barber-shop quartet – the second group could begin the poem behind the first, coming in after the first line: 'belly ache, belly quake'.
- When the children have discussed their ideas, talk about ways in which they could write out their performance. Their 'script' should show who speaks each line.

Task E

- Here repetition and double rhyme are also used to create humour.
- The children, working in pairs, could collect rhyming and onomatopoeic words, borrowing from 'Eyes Bigger Than ...' if necessary, to make simple four-line verses.
- Some children could use the repeating line 'Jelly on a plate', allowing them to focus on the third and fourth lines.

Task F

- The children might like to refer to 'Bubble Trouble' on page 41 of the Pupil Book, and add it to their collection. Also, many nursery rhymes focus on food!

17

Guided Group Work

It's Not Fair *by Christine Potter*
Feet *by Clive Webster (Pupil Book pages 52–55)*

What the Children Need to Know

- Poems can be made from conversation
- Ordinary speech has rhythm
- Repetition can be used to create humour
- Some rhythms skip and bounce in humorous verse

Preparation for Guided Reading

It's Not Fair *page 53*

- The poem could be read in one go, up to 'and she did', with a pause (possibly a moan) then the final line 'it's not fair'.

Feet *page 53*

- The tight rhythm with its full stops after 'feet' helps to give the poem a jerky feel. Read the poem to the children emphasising this.
- See also Task E on page 54 of the Pupil Book for activities relating to the reading of this poem.

My Big Toe Hurts *page 55*

- Ask a child to read the poem aloud, using appropriate expression and intonation.

The Mock Turtle's Song *page 55*

- This extract from the nonsense verse also has a very regular rhythm which bounces along. Repetition and a range of other devices, such as alliteration, are also used to good effect.

Preparation for Guided Writing

Task A

- The children should be able to identify easily with the child in the poem. Some will have experienced the situation themselves. Others might have witnessed a brother or sister in the same situation. However, they might well have varied opinions as to the justice of the case!
- Take the title 'It's Not Fair' and an issue, e.g. bedtime, and ask the children for their views.

Task B

- Collect all the phrases and comments the children use when they are arguing with friends, brothers and sisters and other relatives.
- Suggest they choose some phrases or words to use as repeating lines in a poem of their own, e.g. can/can't, will/won't, yes/no.

Task C

- The tasks here offer a similar process to those in Task B but use double rhyme, i.e. wouldn't/ shouldn't. The rhythm is also 'clumpy'.
- The children can vary the subject, i.e. brother/sister, according to their preferences, as indicated. You might wish to discourage 'friend'!

Task D

- Using the ideas from Task A above, expand to include other issues.
- After discussion, the children can choose an issue and write their poems, using repetition. Some might wish to work in pairs, reading the lines to each other as they progress.

Task F

- Encourage the children to include small details in their poems, such as toenails, as well as the more obvious features of the body!

Task G

- The children might like to model their poem on 'My Big Toe Hurts'. They could begin 'My big/little toe looks like ...'.

Guided Group Work

The Wise Young Owl *by Philip Burton (Pupil Book pages 56–59)*

What the Children Need to Know

- Nonsense verse has its own logic
- Many nursery rhymes are nonsense rhymes
- To be alert to rhyme in poetry
- How to change sentences into the lines of a poem
- A nonsense poem can also be a riddle
- Poems make references to other poems and stories (allusion)
- What common prefixes mean and where to find them

Preparation for Guided Reading

The Wise Young Owl *page 57*

- The poem has a regular rhythm arranged in four-line verses.
- Since it moves along easily you might wish to ask three children to read a verse each. There are frequent pauses at the end of each line and there is sufficient room to allow a pause between each verse. The child reading the last verse should note the abrupt stop (caesura) in the middle of the last line.

The Owl and the Astronaut *page 59*

- The regular rhythm moves this poem along quickly and there are several tricky words, so you might wish to read the poem to the children.
- Note that the poem does not pause until the sixth line, when it comes to an abrupt stop, allowing the voice to fall. The poem divides nicely into two parts.

Preparation for Guided Writing

Task A

- You might wish to discuss how nonsense verse works with some or all of the children before beginning the tasks. (Syntactically the poem makes sense, but semantically it is absurd.)
- Ask the children to shut their eyes and imagine the scenes in the poem (in other words, the reality of the poem). Then ask them how they know it is unreal.

- One way to encourage the children to understand the contradiction is to suggest that nonsense verse comes from pure imagination, like a dream, a fairy story or a nursery rhyme. (Ordinary things happen in a bizarre way, or, if you prefer, vice versa!)

Task B

- 'Yesterday Upon the Stair' presents nonsense as a riddle. You might wish to collect other examples for the children to puzzle out, e.g. 'I fell from the bottom to the top.'

Tasks C and D

- Rhyming successfully is tricky. You could encourage the children to focus on selecting rhymes/words that will also be compatible in meaning, e.g. moon/June. They need use only one pair of rhymes.
- Ask the children where they would place their new verse in the existing poem. (The end of the poem is so neat that it would be better to place the extra verse elsewhere.)

Task E

- The purpose of this task is to stimulate ideas. Once the children understand how to make the sentences and can picture a range of absurd scenes they should be able to think of their own. Some might be able to turn their sentences into poems. A useful way to start is to read the sentences as a series, so the children can hear the lack of metrical structure. Then choose or change lines to accommodate a repeating device to make a poem, e.g.:
  She fried his boots in a paper bag.
  She flew round the sun with a fishing rod.
  … and so on. The last lines of the poem can break the repetition, e.g.:
  While
  Three pink elephants giggled by candlelight.

Task F

- The children might like to collect words with the same prefix, such as 'astro', using a dictionary.
- Encourage the children to create nonsense words and turn them into simple sound poems.
- 'The Owl and the Pussy-Cat' by Edward Lear is available as an activity sheet in these Teacher Notes.

Guided Group Work

A Shaggy Dog Story

by Marian Swinger (Pupil Book pages 60–63)

What the Children Need to Know

- Ideas can be sparked by making associations
- Poems, including nonsense verse, can be stories
- How hyphens can be used to create new words
- A poem can be made from instructions

Preparation for Guided Reading

A Shaggy Dog Story *page 61*

- Three children could read a verse each, observing the pauses and with a slight emphasis on the repeated 'shaggy dog'.
- You might wish to explain what a shaggy dog story is, but it is best done after, rather than before, a first reading.

The Elephant is a Bonnie Bird *page 63*

- This simple nonsense verse delivers its message in a suitably deadpan manner.

Preparation for Guided Writing

Task A

- 'A Shaggy Dog Story' shares several similarities with 'The Wise Young Owl' on page 57 of the Pupil Book: both are nonsense poems, tell a story, involve traditional fantasy settings, defy time and space, have three four-line verses, similar metre, and the end-rhyme pattern (while not the same) shares similarities.
- Encourage the children to notice some of the obvious features.
- Suggestions for discussing what nonsense verse is can be found under Task A of 'The Wise Young Owl'.

Tasks B and C

- You might wish to play the word association game with the children first, before they try it for themselves.
- See 'Nature Shapes' Task C on page 14 of the Pupil Book for suggestions on using the hyphen to create new words.

Task D

- Discuss the features of the mini aeroplane, linking it to the concept of a nonsense poem, i.e. ordinary components are used to make an absurdity.
- You might wish to keep available a collection of illustrations of nonsense machines and creatures. See also Task E on page 63 of the Pupil Book.
- The writing frame (as a series of instructions) provides a form for a poem.

Task E

- You might like to play the following game ('Did you know that moonbeams are really spaghetti?') with the children in preparation for Task E:
    The teacher asks a child: 'Did you know that moonbeams are really …?'
    The child replies with the nonsense answer: '… spaghetti!'
    The same child asks another child a similar question, this time using their own idea: 'Did you know that … are really …?'
    The second child replies with their own nonsense answer, and so on.
  Initially, it does not matter what the replies are. With prompting and praise, the children will gradually make an association between both objects so that the replies become more suitable (as in the case of 'moonbeams' and 'spaghetti' – both are long, thin and white).
- Another useful game – keep separate boxes of interesting verbs, common nouns, pronouns and adjectives. Select one card from each box at random to use as the basis for nonsense sentences, e.g. twirled/sea/he/crimson becomes 'He twirled across the crimson sea.' The best images can be chosen as ideas for writing.
- Encourage the children to imagine that the 'bird creature' in Task E can be made from all sorts of bits and pieces and can do all sorts of unusual things.

Using the Activity Sheets – Part 1

These activity sheets relate primarily to Part 1 of the Pupil Book (pages 4–27) and can be used to support the suggestions for Guided Group Work. However, you might also wish to link the activities to other tasks in the Pupil Book.

Lemon Lollipops

The children are asked to associate groups of words with a sense. It does not matter if they do not understand the meaning of all the words, initially. Their response to the words should be immediate, so that they identify the personal feeling conjured up by the words and translate this into a sentence. This process can help the children to understand more fully what the senses are and their function in poetry. Tasks 4 and 5 introduce the children to the concept of alliteration. The term is not used here and is not introduced until Part 3 in the Pupil Book, but you could introduce the word if you wish.

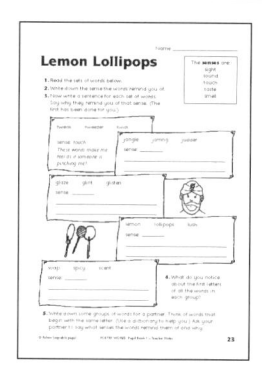

Like Playing Ships

Grasping the idea that a simile compares something with something else is supported by the use of the words 'like' and 'as', and is less abstract than understanding a metaphor.

The simile is one of the most common devices used not only in literature but in ordinary language and the children will almost certainly use it in their talk – point this out. The examples given here relate to everyday experiences, reinforcing this latter point. The children could turn their finished sentences into a poem. The repetition of the present participle and of 'like' and 'as' will help give the poem a unifying quality. Highlight this point for the children – it can often spark the beginning of understanding poetic form. (Please note: some poets do not like the use of 'ing'. I do! It can give energy and rhythm as well as rhyme and I find children relate to its use easily.)

The Jelly-Bus

The hyphen is very useful in writing poetry. It helps the children to connect thoughts and create new words, and emphasises the generative aspects of language. Playing with the words is useful, but the children should also be encouraged to offer definitions. Here they are producing nouns – stress this. Defining nouns also allows the children to think of imaginative ideas more easily, since common nouns are concrete and give scope for interesting visual images. You might find that the children want to offer definitions for more than six words. Encourage them to create their own words to hyphenate, and to find ready-made ones in a dictionary.

Beautiful Letters

There is often a difficulty with producing calligrams and shape poems. Children can very easily end up decorating words with pictures that take their fancy, or with popular symbols, without much regard to the meaning of a word or words. Yet thinking visually and spatially is fundamental to writing shape poems. The activity sheet suggests experimenting with a range of approaches and emphasises meaning. You can then guide the children in whichever way you wish. Calligrams (in which the whole word is presented pictorially) are a good place to start. Writing a fully formed shape poem is more difficult than it appears and the children should be encouraged to settle on something that is manageable in both meaning and representation. The example given, the 'storm' poem, involves only two shapes but generates sufficient vocabulary and is simple enough to be within the scope of most children. Making a list of relevant words first is also useful.

21

Using the Activity Sheets – Part 1

Spin Me a Rhyme

This activity sheet provides the children with the opportunity to practise identifying rhyming words (and, of course, non-rhyming words). The work can be used as an introduction to rhyme pattern (which is discussed more fully in Pupil Book 2). Although end rhyme is one of the most common forms of rhyme, and one which most of us associate with poetry, other forms of rhyme are also important in comic verse. Ask the children if they can identify any words in the middle of a line, in the chant, which rhyme with any others, e.g. 'flea' in line five rhymes with 'tea' at the end of line four. While this is not internal rhyme here, it introduces a broader idea of rhyme. An example of internal rhyme might be 'A cup of tea for you and me', which you could discuss in the context of this particular poem.

'No!'

Thomas Hood was one of the most popular poets of the nineteenth century. 'No!' is printed here in its complete form, for those children who might be interested in reading it. It is quite challenging for today's children but they can still enjoy the repetition and use of punctuation and might wish to perform the poem, using the punctuation as a guide. Unfamiliar vocabulary and expressions, apart from those mentioned, might be: 't'other side the way', 'locomotion', 'notion', 'gentility', 'nobility', 'healthful ease'. You might wish to discuss them with the children beforehand or let them simply read the poem for themselves.

Four Creatures

This is an easier poem. Most children should be able to guess the intended answers to the riddles, and might also present other reasonable answers, such as:

verse 1	tiger or a member of the cat family, or any other creature with fur, claws and teeth
verse 2	hawk, or any other bird of prey, besides the eagle
verse 3	other tropical fish (or wind-up fish, used in the bath, from which the idea came!)
verse 4	snail

The children might wish to perform the poem. The repetition of 'its' and 'is its' can be tricky.

Lemon Lollipops

Name _____

The **senses** are:
   sight
   sound
   touch
   taste
   smell

1. Read the sets of words below.
2. Write down the sense the words remind you of.
3. Now write a sentence for each set of words.
   Say why they remind you of that sense.
   (The first has been done for you.)

---

tweak   tweezer   twist

sense: *touch*
These words make me feel as if someone is pinching me!

---

jangle   jarring   judder

sense: _____
_____
_____

---

glaze   glint   glisten

sense: _____
_____
_____

---

lemon   lollipops   lush

sense: _____
_____
_____

---

soap   spicy   scent

sense: _____
_____
_____

4. What do you notice about the first letters of all the words in each group?

5. Write down some groups of words for a partner. Think of words that begin with the same letter. (Use a dictionary to help you.) Ask your partner to say what senses the words remind them of and why.

© Folens (copiable page)   POETRY WORKS Pupil Book 1 – Teacher Notes   23

Name _____

Like Playing Ships

Sometimes we love the jobs we have to do.
Sometimes we hate them.
Washing the dishes is *like playing ships in the bath.*
Scrubbing the oven is *as hard as fighting a giant.*

A **simile** uses 'like' or 'as'.

Finish these sentences using 'like' or 'as'.

1. Tidying my room is _____ .

2. Clearing out the car is _____ .

3. Walking the dog is _____ .

4. Pushing the supermarket trolley is _____ .

5. Cleaning the rabbit's hutch is _____ .

6. Cooking the tea is _____ .

7. Bathing the baby is _____ .

8. Combing the cat is _____ .

Add two more sentences about the jobs people do in your home.
Use 'like' or 'as'.

9. _____ .

10. _____ .

The Jelly-Bus

Name _____

1. Read these words which are joined by hyphens:

| jelly-bus   hop-giggle |

A **hyphen** joins two words.

2. Now try joining these words in different ways. How many new words can you make? Write down your new words below.

bus	jelly	squelch
bubble	twirl	rap
jam	giggle	clown
bat	straw	hop
balloon	smile	bike
pan	ribbon	squash

_____
_____
_____
_____

3. Choose the six new words you like best. Think of meanings for them.

A jelly-bus could be a party bus.
A hop-giggle could be a loud hiccup.

4. Share your new words with your group.

Name _____

Beautiful Letters

keywords
calligram
shape poem

1. Look at these calligrams. Can you see how the letters show the meaning of each word?

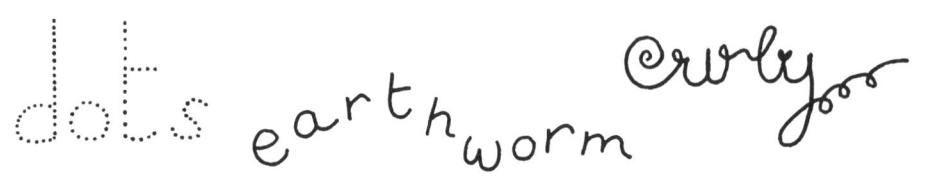

dots   earthworm   curly

2. Here the letters become pictures, which also show the word's meaning.

PAINTING

3. This shape poem uses lots of words to show its meaning.

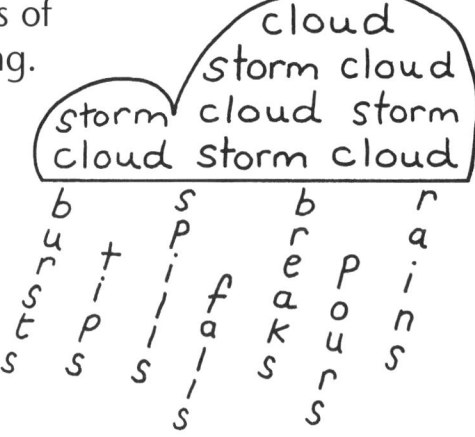

cloud
storm cloud
storm cloud storm
cloud storm cloud

bursts spits spills falls breaks pours rains

4. Turn these words into calligrams or shape words.

bounce   swimming   bigger   hole   round   note   yawn   pie   sport

5. Write a shape poem. Choose one of the ideas below or think of your own.

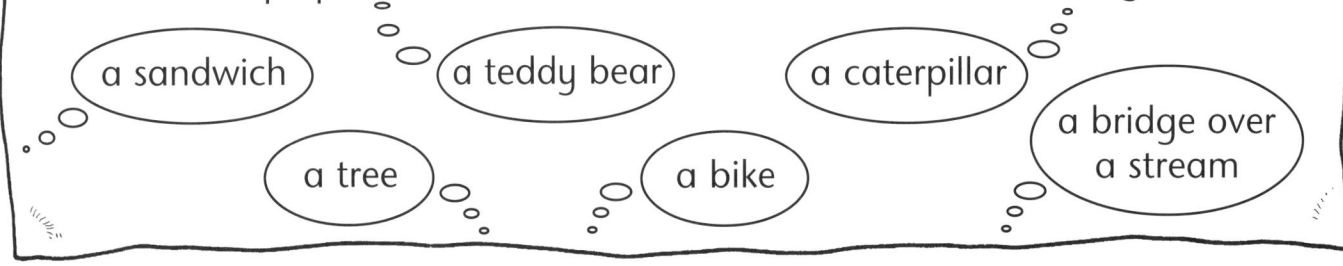

a sandwich   a teddy bear   a caterpillar   a bridge over a stream
a tree   a bike

26   POETRY WORKS Pupil Book 1 – Teacher Notes   © Folens (copiable page)

Spin Me a Rhyme

Name _____

1. Circle the words that rhyme in each line. The first has been done for you.

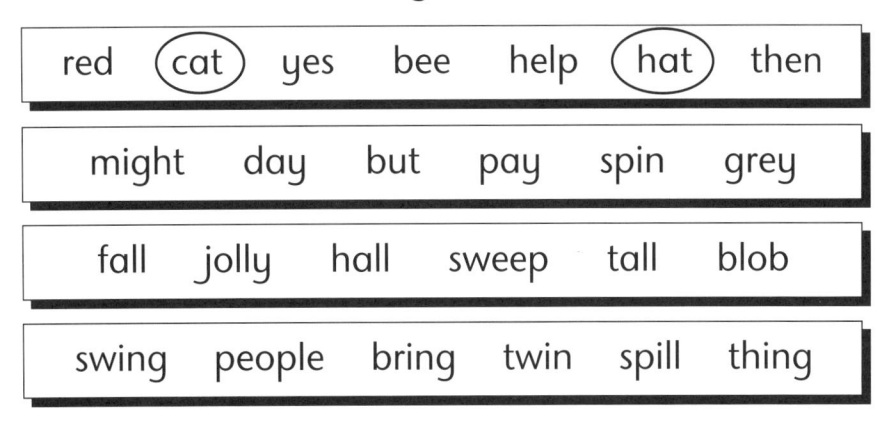

| red | (cat) | yes | bee | help | (hat) | then |

| might | day | but | pay | spin | grey |

| fall | jolly | hall | sweep | tall | blob |

| swing | people | bring | twin | spill | thing |

keywords
rhyme
verse

2. Read this playground chant.

> One, two, three,
> Mother caught a flea;
> She put it in the teapot,
> To make a cup of tea.
>
> The flea jumped out,
> Mother gave a shout!
> Here comes Father,
> With his shirt hanging out!

3. Circle the rhyming words in the chant.

4. Think of other words that rhyme with those in the chant. Write them down below.

More rhyming words	
verse 1	**verse 2**

No!

The nineteenth-century poet Thomas Hood (1799–1845) was born in London. His father was a bookseller so he knew all about books. Thomas became a writer and poet and wrote for newspapers and magazines. His poems were very popular with the public.

Here is the complete poem 'No!'.

> **No!**
>
> No sun – no moon!
> No morn – no noon –
> No dawn – no dusk – no proper time of day –
> No sky – no earthly view –
> No distance looking blue –
> No road – no street – no 't'other side the way' –
> No end to any Row –
> No indications where the Crescents go –
> No top to any steeple –
> No recognitions of familiar people –
> No courtesies for showing 'em!
> No knowing 'em! –
> No travelling at all – no locomotion,
> No inkling of the way – no notion –
> 'No go' – by land or ocean –
> No mail – no post –
> No news from any foreign coast –
> No Park – no Ring – no afternoon gentility –
> No company – no nobility –
> No warmth, no cheerfulness, no healthful ease,
> No comfortable feel in any member –
> No shade, no shine, no butterflies, no bees,
> No fruits, no flowers, no leaves, no birds –
> **November!**
>
> *Thomas Hood*

t' – the
'em – them
member – arm or leg

Things to think about

1. What was the weather like as the poet wrote his poem?
2. How do the dashes make you read the poem?
3. How would you say 'November!' at the end? How does that final word make you feel?

28   POETRY WORKS Pupil Book 1 – Teacher Notes   © Folens (copiable page)

Four Creatures

Name _____

Four Creatures

Soft is its fur,
Sharp its claw,
Sharp is its tooth,
Soft its paw.

Swift is its wing,
Firm its eye,
Firm is its clutch,
Swift its cry.

Gold is its tail,
Fast its pace,
Fast is its fin,
Gold its face.

Slow is its foot,
Hard its back,
Hard is its journey,
Slow its track.

Mary Green

Things to think about

1. Can you guess what the four creatures are? (Check at the bottom of the page.)
2. What other creatures could they be?
3. What do you notice about the first word of each line?

Answers: cat, eagle, goldfish, tortoise.

Using the Activity Sheets – Part 2

These activity sheets relate primarily to Part 2 of the Pupil Book (pages 28–39) and can be used to support the suggestions for Guided Group Work. However, you might also wish to link the activities to other tasks in the Pupil Book.

Animal Acrostics

Acrostics are harder to write than they look, since the word/s in each line must relate to the vertical meaning – children sometimes forget this. Words beginning with a vowel can prove the most difficult; consequently all the vertical words provided are short, with only one vowel in most cases. Try to bear this in mind when the children create their own acrostics. Writing acrostics will help develop the children's quick recall of vocabulary (have a dictionary and a thesaurus available). Some children might be able to use each word as a starter for a line of poetry, as in 'Caribbean' on page 29 of the Pupil Book. Others could emphasise adjectives for describing the word. For example:

> Pretty pink porker
> In the farmyard
> Gorgeous and greedy

Tapping Out the Beat, Stressing the Words, Going With the Flow, Finding the Best Voice

It is suggested that these activity sheets are used in conjunction with each other as they all relate to rhythm and stress. Children sometimes confuse 'rhyme' and 'rhythm' since the two can work closely together in verses that use lots of rhyme and have a strong rhythm (such as nursery rhymes).

Tapping Out the Beat

The children are asked to identify the number of syllables in a word, ranging from one to three. You might wish to ensure that the children can clearly distinguish between a syllable and a word. They could add further verses, sayings or songs that they know and work out the syllable patterns. (For the present, it does not matter if the children overemphasise the syllables – it might help them to count more easily. Issues relating to stressed and unstressed syllables are dealt with on the following activity sheet.)

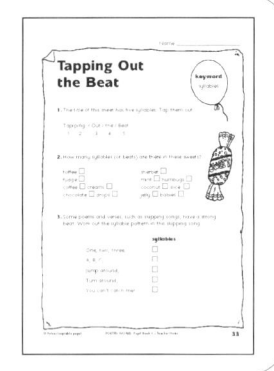

Stressing the Words

Discuss with the children how we stress words in normal conversation according to the meaning we give them. Develop this into a discussion of expression in poetry. Once the children have completed Task 1, talk about how the meaning of what they are saying alters – quite dramatically in some cases. When they read the playground chant, this becomes even more marked. (Ask them to stress 'me' then 'you', in the last line of each verse.) This activity sheet also offers the opportunity to distinguish between rhyme and rhythm.

Using the Activity Sheets – Part 2

Going With the Flow

'Sampan' is an excellent poem for reading aloud and creating a dream-like feeling and sound. All the lines of the poem run into each other, emphasising both the flow of words and the sounds of the river. The onomatopoeia, in particular, shows how a poem might be read without overstressing the syllables and yet making their presence felt. You might wish to ask the children to draw up a list of suitable 'sea sounds' as well as words, and to share them with each other before writing their poems. They can of course repeat lines and not all the sounds need be dreamy. A seagull's 'cark, cark' for instance can successfully jar against the sound of the sand and sea. Nonetheless, you might find the children feel sleepy after reading their poems to each other!

Finding the Best Voice

The three contrasting poems on this activity sheet provide the children with the opportunity to practise reading in a variety of voices.

The Little Moon has a gentle, sinking rhythm. This is encouraged by the pauses, the alliteration using the letter 's', the use of vocabulary such as 'little', and the image of the moon sinking out of sight. Note also how the run-on line '… the little moon/Drops down …' draws the poem to a close.

The Beetroot has a bouncy, matter-of-fact rhythm and a throwaway final word ('dinnegar'), which a child might say. In this respect it is like a nursery rhyme. The metre is regular and the heavy use of assonance in lines one and three (the internal vowel rhyme ee/ea) helps to keep the voice steady, contrasting with the bouncier lines two and four.

Wonderful Prairie has an irregular rhythm and the lack of end rhyme accentuates the free verse. The poem is a statement of wonder about the dawn.

What a Performance!

The children can use the Scottish charm provided to practise what they have learned about reading aloud. You might wish to discuss particular features with them first: who might read what, how they might modulate their voices between verses, as well as having a brief discussion on actions, instruments and props.

What is Spiky?

On this activity sheet, the children are encouraged to explore the range of meanings in an adjective – related to the senses. You could prompt them to think of senses and feelings to prompt the choice of nouns. For example:

grumbling ⟶ sound ⟶ stomach
grumbling ⟶ emotion ⟶ mum/dad/teacher
grumbling ⟶ sight ⟶ frown

The poem given as an example, 'Spiky', offers a form that the children can work with. The adjective at the end closes the lines and also accentuates the meaning of the original adjective, through contrast.

Name _____

Animal Acrostics

keywords
acrostic
dictionary

1. Read these acrostics.

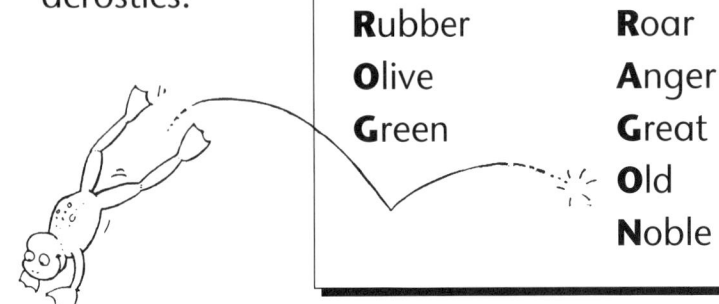

Flippers   **D**azzle
Rubber   **R**oar
Olive   **A**nger
Green   **G**reat
                  Old
                  Noble

2. What words are made by the first letters, when you read down? Write them here.

_____

_____

3. All the words in an acrostic are linked in meaning. What word does this acrostic make? Write it down.

Dear
Old
Goldie

_____

4. Complete these acrostics. Remember, choose words that are linked in meaning. Use a dictionary if you need to.

C _____   C _____   P _____
O _____   A _____   E _____
W _____   T _____   T _____
                                          S _____

H _____   S _____
E _____   N _____
N _____   A _____
                     K _____
                     E _____

5. Invent your own acrostics.

32   POETRY WORKS Pupil Book 1 – Teacher Notes   © Folens (copiable page)

Tapping Out the Beat

keyword

syllables

1. The title of this sheet has five syllables. Tap them out:

Tap/ping / Out / the / Beat
  1   2   3   4   5

2. How many syllables (or beats) are there in these sweets? (The first has been done for you.)

toffee [2]   sherbet □
fudge □   mint □ humbugs □
coffee □ creams □   coconut □ slice □
chocolate □ drops □ jelly □ babies □

3. Some poems and verses, such as skipping songs, have a strong beat. Work out the syllable pattern in this skipping song.

	syllables
One, two, three,	□
A, B, C,	□
Jump around,	□
Turn around,	□
You can't catch me!	□

Stressing the Words

keywords
syllable
rhythm

1. Read the following, stressing the words or syllables in capital letters.

   Be QUICK!   Let's go NOW!
   We CAN'T come!   REAlly!

2. Now say them this way.

   BE quick!   Let's GO now!
   WE can't come!   ReaLLY!

3. What sayings do you use at home? What words do you stress? Write down a saying with the word or syllable you stress in capital letters.

   _____
   _____

4. Now stress the saying in another way. (You could stress more than one word or syllable.)

   _____
   _____

5. Beat and stress make up the rhythm of a poem. Here are both verses of the skipping song 'One, Two, Three'. Say it, stressing the words in different ways.

One, two, three,	Four, five, six,
A, B, C,	Got you in a fix,
Jump around,	Jump around,
Turn around,	Turn around,
You can't catch me!	You can't catch me!

6. Can you remember the difference between rhythm and rhyme? Find out.

Going With the Flow

1. Read 'Sampan'.
2. Although the poem has a strong beat it also has a sleepy feeling. Practise reading the poem without overstressing the syllables or beat.

Sampan

Waves lap lap
Fish fins clap clap
Brown sails flap flap
Chop-sticks tap tap
Up and down the long green river
Ohe Ohe lanterns quiver
Willow branches touch the river
Ohe Ohe lanterns quiver
Waves lap lap
Fish fins clap clap
Brown sails flap flap
Chop-sticks tap tap

Tao Lang Pee

keyword
syllable

3. Write your own poem about the sea. You might be on the beach at the end of a sunny day. The tide could be coming in. What sounds would you hear? How would you feel? Read the beginning of this poem to help you.

The little waves curl *drift drift*
The sand slips back *shift shift*
A seagull _____

_____
_____
_____
_____

© Folens (copiable page)   POETRY WORKS Pupil Book 1 – Teacher Notes   35

Finding the Best Voice

Name _____

1. Read these three poems.

keywords
syllable
rhythm

The Little Moon

The night is come, but not too soon,
And sinking silently,
All silently, the little moon
Drops down behind the sky.

H.W. Longfellow

The Beetroot

The beetroot is a sorry beast,
He paddles around in vinegar,
Gets eaten for a tea-time feast,
Or someone's pickled dinnegar.

Wonderful Prairie

Wonderful prairie,
Golden-haired,
Swinging on the sun-curve,
Before even a mouse stirs.

2. Answer these three questions.

Which poem has a bouncy rhythm? _____

Which has a soft rhythm? _____

Which has an irregular rhythm? _____

3. Practise reading the poems. Which words do you stress? How does the punctuation help you?

4. Decide the best way to read each poem and read them to a partner.

36   POETRY WORKS Pupil Book 1 – Teacher Notes   © Folens (copiable page)

What a Performance!

1. Read this Scottish charm or spell. It is like a performance poem.

Struthill Well

Three white stones,
And three black pins,
Three yellow gowans
Off the green,

Into the well,
With a one, two, three,
And a fortune, a fortune,
Come to me.

Anon

gowans – daisies

2. What is the charm about? What does it ask the reader to do? Write your answer down, then tell a friend in your own words.

_____

_____

_____

_____

3. How could you perform it? How many people would be needed?

_____

_____

4. What musical instruments and other props could you use to perform the poem? Make a list on the back of the sheet. Remember, you can use all kinds of things to make sounds and shapes.

5. Share your list with a partner. Between you choose the best things from your lists and work out how you will perform the poem. (Try not to use too many props.)

6. Perform the poem to a group.

What is Spiky?

Name _____

keywords
adjective
dictionary
thesaurus

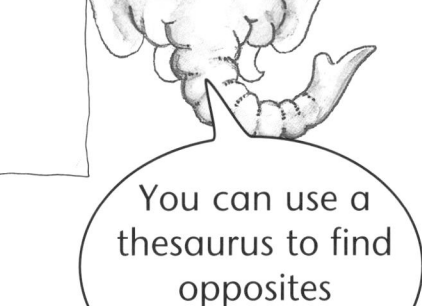

1. Read this poem.

Spiky

A spiky hedgehog
A spiky haircut
A spiky shoe
A spiky mood
And – a sleek cat.

REMEMBER

You can use a thesaurus to find opposites (antonyms).

2. The adjectives below can be used to write poems. First think of different nouns to go with each one. Then add an opposite adjective for the last line, as in 'Spiky'.

growling	drowsy	hard	slippery
_____	_____	____	_____
_____	_____	____	_____
_____	_____	____	_____
_____	_____	____	_____
_____	_____	____	_____
_____	_____	____	_____

3. Check the meanings of any adjectives you do not know in a dictionary. Write down several nouns and then choose the best ones.

4. Now use your lists to write four poems.

POETRY WORKS Pupil Book 1 – Teacher Notes © Folens (copiable page)

Using the Activity Sheets – Part 3

These activity sheets relate primarily to Part 3 of the Pupil Book (pages 40–63) and can be used to support the suggestions for Guided Group Work. However, you might also wish to link the activities to other tasks in the Pupil Book.

Making Tongue Twisters

This activity can be fun to do and helps the children to understand the nature of alliteration and how it can be used to create effects. It also provides the children with words that they can use to start writing their own tongue twisters. (Point out that there are two sounds used in the tongue twisters in Task 2.) Explain to the children that the words can be changed from nouns to adjectives, and so on, as they please. The children might also wish to supply words of their own for Task 3. You could provide examples of tongue twisters to help them get started:

Plenty of peppered parsnips and porridge, please.
Five furry frogs fiddling in a frosty fuss.

The children might wish to collect tongue twisters from anthologies.

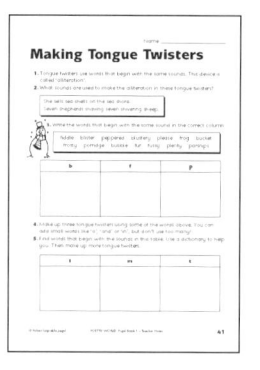

Using Sounds Carefully

This activity addresses the use of alliteration in more serious poetry; children can sometimes assume that alliteration is to be found only in comic verse, when in fact it is one of the most common devices used. Remind the children to circle only those letters that come at the beginning of words (and not, for example, the 'w' in 'stalwart'). There are fewer words beginning 'g' and 'l' – both are in 'Barbara Ellen' (green/Green, lay/love). Furthermore 'l' receives support from the 'll' consonants in 'All', 'swelling', 'Ellen' and 'William'. Remind the children to treat each verse separately. The 'trick question' in Task 4 focuses on the word 'one' that has a beginning sound 'w'. Use this example to remind the children that it is the sound and not the letter in alliteration that matters.

Only Joking!

These jokes might help the children to understand what a 'play on words' is. The first uses a pun (in so far as 'ear' sounds like "ere" which is slang for 'here') and is quite easy to understand. Remind the children of this joke if they forget what a pun is – 'Knock, knock' jokes fulfil the same purpose. The remaining jokes depend on either lateral thinking or word association. 'My Sister' can be identified as having rhythm. It rhymes too, but you might wish to point out that this is not always a feature of poetry.

Silly Sounds

Onomatopoeia is often the poetic device that appeals to children most – it's not difficult to see why! Children generate their own onomatopoeic words easily, in play and conversation. In the first task they are asked to match the words, mostly by half rhyme. (This activity could also be used to illustrate half rhyme.) Further tasks are more adventurous and ask the children to match the words in other ways. This is a good activity for generating more onomatopoeic vocabulary, with the newly-created words often producing instant connotations in the mind. (This task also points out the usefulness of the hyphen.) The term 'onomatopoeia' is not used here, but you might like to mention it.

39

Using the Activity Sheets – Part 3

Loves Hates Always Never

This is a variation on the well-known 'I love/hate …' framework to help the children write nonsense poetry. The certainty of 'love' and 'hate' is juxtaposed against the absurd second half of the line, as though it were really true. You might like to discuss how the children could finish their poems before they tackle the sheet on their own, e.g. creating a verse that diverges from the pattern: 'We love …'. Discuss with the children how their poems are best read or performed.

Which is Which?

In this activity, the children are asked to distinguish between a (traditional and well-loved) cautionary tale, 'If You Should Meet a Crocodile'; a simple shape poem, 'sky-high-floor' (which can be read either way according to whether you are travelling up or down); an acrostic, 'Bubble' and a joke.

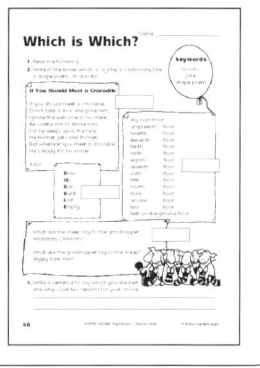

The Owl and the Pussy-Cat

Many of the children will know this poem and will enjoy reading it. The poem is printed here so that the children can refer to it when completing page 59 of the Pupil Book, which discusses 'The Owl and the Astronaut' by Gareth Owen and in which the same owl and pussy-cat are referred to.

Name _____

Making Tongue Twisters

1. Tongue twisters use words that begin with the same sounds. This device is called 'alliteration'.

2. What sounds are used to make the alliteration in these tongue twisters?

> She sells sea-shells on the sea shore.
> Seven shepherds shaving seven shivering sheep.

3. Write the words that begin with the same sound in the correct column.

> fiddle   blister   peppered   blustery   please   frog   bucket
> frosty   porridge   bubble   fur   fussy   plenty   parsnips

b	f	p

4. Make up three tongue twisters using some of the words above. You can add small words like 'a', 'and' or 'in', but don't use too many!

5. Find words that begin with the sounds in this table. Use a dictionary to help you. Then make up more tongue twisters.

l	m	t

© Folens (copiable page)   POETRY WORKS Pupil Book 1 – Teacher Notes   41

Name _____

Using Sounds Carefully

1. Read these verses. They use alliteration carefully but are not comic verse.

From **The Wife of Usher's Well**

There lived a wife at Usher's Well,
And a wealthy wife was she;
She had three stout and stalwart sons,
And sent them over the sea.

Traditional

stalwart – strong

From **Barbara Ellen**

All in the merry month of May,
When the green buds they were swelling,
Young William Green on his death-bed lay,
For the love of Barbara Ellen.

Traditional

2. Circle the beginning sounds in each verse that are repeated.

3. Now complete the table below. Tick all the beginning sounds that are repeated for each verse.

	Beginning sounds							
	g	l	m	s	w			
The Wife of Usher's Well								
Barbara Ellen								

4. Add this poem to your table and tick the beginning sounds that are repeated. But be careful! It is easy to make a mistake in the last line.

Grey Goose and Gander

Grey goose and gander,
Waft your wings together,
And carry the good king's daughter
Over the one strand river.

Anon

42   POETRY WORKS Pupil Book 1 – Teacher Notes   © Folens (copiable page)

Only Joking!

Name _____

keyword
joke

1. Read these jokes.

> What did the teacher say to the elephant? *Listen ear!*

> If you were given 50p and lost 20p, what would you have? *30p, of course. (You thought I'd say a hole in your pocket, didn't you?)*

> **My Sister**
>
> She cleans her teeth with ketchup,
> She's never missed a day,
> It makes her teeth like Dracula's,
> And frightens Aunty May.

> **Tired Jokes**
>
> What fish is always asleep?
> *A kipper!*
>
> What should you say to a yawning lion?
> *Lion the sofa!*

> What do you get if you cross a crab-apple with strong cheese? *A bad tummy!*

2. Which is a joke poem? How can you tell? Write down your answer.

_____

_____

3. Find out what these are.

| shanks's pony | a hot cross bun | a yak | a woolly mammoth |

4. With a partner, choose two phrases from the box above and try turning them into jokes. Remember, the words can have double meanings. Tell your joke to an adult.

Silly Sounds

Name _____

1. Match the words in the box that go together best and write them down, like this:

   hipperty-hopperty

flip	patter
click	lumperty
pitter	slop
squiggle	flap
twing	gurdy
thumperty	wiggle
hurdy	clack
slip	twang

2. What do the new words remind you of? Think about each one.
3. On the back of the sheet match the words in other ways, thinking about what new meaning they could have, like this:

   hopperty-flip ⟶ This could be someone doing a cartwheel!

   Try to make ten new words. You can use a word more than once.
4. Talk to a partner about what your new words could mean.

Name _____

Loves Hates Always Never

keywords
nonsense poem
repeating pattern

1. With a partner, write a nonsense poem, using the repeating pattern 'loves, hates, always, never'. Write a line each, using the beginning lines below. Think of silly things! The first has been started for you.

A baby ant loves to hear lullabies
A baby ant hates to eat pickles
A baby ant always _____
A baby ant never _____

A long-haired giraffe loves _____
A long-haired giraffe hates _____
A long-haired giraffe always _____
A long-haired giraffe never _____

An over-sized sock loves _____
An over-sized sock hates _____
An over-sized sock always _____
An over-sized sock never _____

2. Now think of an example (an animal or an object) for your partner and ask them to complete it on their own.
3. Give your poems titles.
4. Practise reading your poems to each other.

© Folens (copiable page)   POETRY WORKS Pupil Book 1 – Teacher Notes   **45**

Which is Which?

Name _____

1. Read the following.
2. Write in the boxes which is: a joke, a cautionary tale, a shape poem, an acrostic.

keywords
acrostic
joke
shape poem

If You Should Meet a Crocodile

If you should meet a crocodile,
Don't take a stick and poke him;
Ignore the welcome in his smile,
Be careful not to stroke him.
For he sleeps upon the Nile,
He thinner gets and thinner;
But whene'er you meet a crocodile
He's ready for his dinner.

Anon

Blow
Up
Ball
Burst
Lost
Empty

sky-high-floor
umpteenth   floor
twelfth   floor
eleventh   floor
tenth   floor
ninth   floor
eighth   floor
seventh   floor
sixth   floor
fifth   floor
fourth   floor
third   floor
second   floor
first   floor
feet-on-the-ground-floor

What did the sheep say to the grasshopper?
Meeeeeery Christmas!

What did the grasshopper say to the sheep?
Hoppy New Year!

3. Write a sentence to say which you like best and why. Give two reasons for your choice.

_____

_____

Name _____

The Owl and the Pussy-Cat

Edward Lear (1812–1888) wrote poetry about strange creatures and people. This is one of his most popular poems.

The Owl and the Pussy-Cat

The Owl and the Pussy-Cat went to sea
    In a beautiful pea-green boat,
They took some honey, and plenty of money,
    Wrapped up in a five-pound note.
The Owl looked up to the stars above,
    And sang to a small guitar,
"O lovely Pussy! O Pussy, my love,
    What a beautiful Pussy you are,
        You are,
        You are!
    What a beautiful Pussy you are!"

Pussy said to the Owl, "You elegant fowl!
    How charmingly sweet you sing!
O let us be married! too long we have tarried:
    But what shall we do for a ring?"
They sailed away for a year and a day,
    To the land where the Bong-Tree grows,
And there in a wood a Piggy-wig stood,
    With a ring at the end of his nose,
        His nose,
        His nose,
    With a ring at the end of his nose.

"Dear Pig, are you willing to sell for one shilling
    "Your ring?" Said the Piggy, "I will."
So they took it away, and were married next day
    By the Turkey who lives on the hill.
They dined on mince, and slices of quince,
    Which they ate with a runcible spoon;
And hand in hand, on the edge of the sand,
    They danced by the light of the moon,
        The moon,
        The moon,
    They danced by the light of the moon.

Edward Lear

---

tarried – waited
shilling – a coin no longer used
quince – a fruit
runcible spoon – one of Edward Lear's own nonsense words for a fork, curved like a spoon.

Things to think about

People often want to sing and dance when they read this poem. Why do you think this is?

Sound patterns and metre

The following are examples of common sound patterns in English verse. It is not suggested that you use this sheet to teach from directly, but that you keep it for reference. The examples are presented using the Consonant, Vowel, Consonant (CVC) formula. (This is a strict formula and many people accommodate variations, particularly with consonance and alliteration.) The letters in bold indicate the sounds concerned. It is important to remember that it is the sounds that matter and not the spelling.

CVC (full rhyme)	cat/hat	bluff/tough	kite/plight
C**V**C (half rhyme or consonance)	ten/sun	mend/wind	crept/slipped
C**V**C (slant rhyme or off rhyme)	pin/pun	twing/twang	rule/rail
CVC (reverse rhyme)	sit/sip	trap/tram	friend/frenzy
C**V**C (assonance)	pen/met	train/sail	stream/beak
CVC (alliteration)	live/long	butter/bought	such/sorrow

Double rhyme has an unstressed syllable followed by a stressed syllable:

    puddle/muddle

Triple rhymes and rhymes with multiple unstressed syllables are often used in comic verse:

    geography/topography   manipulation/stipulation

Rhymes can occur at various points in the verse or line. Here is an example of a double rhyme as an internal rhyme:

    He stepped in a puddle right up to his middle.

Metre
Traditionally, the rhythms of English poetry or the regular patterns of stressed (/) and unstressed (x) syllables are referred to as metre and the lines of a verse have units within them called feet. There are also variations within this. (Not all poets like this system, partly because the metrical foot does not adequately express rhythm in all its subtlety and variation.)

    x / = iambic   x x / = anapaest   / x = trochee   / x x = dactyl   / / = spondee
    1 foot = monometer   2 feet = dimeter   3 feet = trimeter   4 feet = tetrameter
    5 feet = pentameter   6 feet = hexameter   7 feet = heptameter … and so on.

Iambic pentameter is usually referred to as the most common metre in English:

    The **plough**man **home**ward **plods** his **wea**ry **way**.*
     x   /   x   /   x   /   x   /   x   /

Note how the stress suits the meaning of the line.

(*From 'Elegy Written in a Country Churchyard' by Thomas Gray.)